Original title:

The Art of Feeling Without Words

Copyright © 2024 Creative Arts Management OÜ

All rights reserved.

Author: Robert Ashford

ISBN HARDBACK: 978-9916-90-758-0

ISBN PAPERBACK: 978-9916-90-759-7

The Breath Between Us

In whispers soft, our secrets flow,
A fragile thread that seems to glow.
Beneath the stars, where silence dwells,
The breath between us gently swells.

With every heartbeat, time slows down,
A sacred space where dreams abound.
In the stillness, love's spark ignites,
A dance of shadows in moonlight sights.

Hues of Unvoiced Longing

In colors deep, emotions blend,
A canvas brushed with whispers penned.
Each hue a word we dare not speak,
In every glance, the truth we seek.

From crimson blush to azure sigh,
The palette paints what hearts imply.
In silent strokes, our stories weave,
A tapestry of hope, believe.

Echoes of the Unsayable

In shadows cast by fleeting light,
The echoes linger, soft as night.
Words unspoken hang in the air,
A melody of hearts laid bare.

Through the silence, a longing calls,
In secret chambers, desire sprawls.
Each glance exchanged, a fleeting chance,
An unsaid truth in a silent dance.

Silent Symphony of Souls

A symphony where silence reigns,
In the stillness, love's refrain.
Each note a heartbeat, soft and clear,
Resounding truths we hold most dear.

In harmony, our spirits sing,
The beauty found in everything.
With every pause, a story shared,
In silent verses, souls declared.

Muffled Songs of the Heart

Whispers drift in twilight air,
Softly woven dreams laid bare.
Quiet fears and tender sighs,
Love's echo in the night's disguise.

Laughter dances on the breeze,
Secret moments, hearts at ease.
In shadows, memories entwine,
Muffled songs, your heart with mine.

Emotions Wrapped in Stillness

In quiet corners, feelings dwell,
Stories untold, they softly swell.
The weight of silence holds them tight,
As stars emerge to greet the night.

Reflection pools like gentle streams,
Carrying the weight of dreams.
Layered thoughts, a soft embrace,
In stillness, find a sacred space.

Clarity in the Chaos of Silence

Amidst the noise, a moment found,
A whispered truth, profound, unbound.
In chaos, souls begin to see,
The clarity of what will be.

Silence speaks, its voice so clear,
Navigating what we hold dear.
In the hush, a guiding light,
Bringing order to the night.

Quiet Expressions in the Night

Moonlight spills on muted streams,
Casting shadows on our dreams.
In the dark, emotions flow,
Quiet expressions, hearts aglow.

With every sigh, the world stands still,
Moments cherished, gently thrill.
In night's embrace, we find our way,
Whispers of love in soft array.

Ephemeral Touch

A fleeting glance beneath the stars,
Whispers of love that fade like mist.
In twilight's glow, we share our scars,
Moments that fade, yet still persist.

Soft fingers brush as time slips by,
A gentle warmth in evening's hush.
In memory's vault, they never die,
Yet in the now, we feel the crush.

Eternal Embrace

In every heartbeat, rhythms blend,
A shelter found in open arms.
Though seasons change, this love won't end,
Forever safe from worldly harms.

Through stormy nights and blazing days,
Our bond, a flame that never wanes.
In every look, a thousand rays,
A promise kept through joy and pains.

The Artistry of the Unsung

In shadows cast where whispers dwell,
A beauty found in silent grace.
The stories wrapped in tales we tell,
Unseen, they leave a soft embrace.

With every note, a heart awakes,
An artist's touch in simple lines.
In quiet moments, courage makes,
A canvas filled with unseen signs.

Adrift in Silent Reverie

Upon the waves of thoughts unknown,
I drift through realms of dreams unchained.
In quietude, my heart has grown,
A sanctuary, joy uncontained.

Each moment lingers, soft and sweet,
As stars align in cosmic dance.
In stillness, echoes gently greet,
A wanderer's heart in whispered trance.

Timelessness in a Whisper

A secret shared in hushed tones low,
A fleeting word, a spark ignites.
In gentle breaths, old stories flow,
Across the fabric of the nights.

With every sigh, a world unfolds,
In echoes of the past, we find.
A whispered truth that never folds,
Timeless threads that bind the mind.

Silent Sonnet

In the stillness where whispers fade,
Words unspoken in shadows laid.
Time drifts softly like autumn leaves,
Captured moments, the heart believes.

A gentle echo, a lingering sigh,
Promises linger, yet days slip by.
In silence, bonds are tightly spun,
A sonnet written, but never done.

Flesh and Memory

In the warm embrace of faded touch,
Skin remembers, feeling so much.
Moments etched in delicate lines,
Flesh and memory, intertwining signs.

The past dances in twilight's glow,
Fragrant whispers like seeds we sow.
In every heartbeat, echoes remain,
A tapestry woven with joy and pain.

The Language of Touch

Fingers tracing a timeless script,
In every caress, a world eclipsed.
Soft as shadows, weightless and free,
The language of touch speaks quietly.

Each stroke a story, every sigh a plea,
A dialogue whispered, just you and me.
In the space between heartbeats, we find,
The unspoken bond, beautifully blind.

Shadows of Sorrow

Beneath the moon's soft and solemn light,
Shadows gather, cloaked in night.
Whispers of sorrow drift through the trees,
Carried by winds like forgotten pleas.

Every tear that falls to the ground,
In silence, echoes a heart that's bound.
Yet from the darkness, hope takes flight,
Emerging slowly, reclaiming the light.

Hidden Wavelengths of Affection

In swirling light, your laughter glows,
A silent dance where soft winds blow.
In subtle shades our hearts align,
We weave a bond that feels divine.

Beneath the stars, we gently sway,
In muted tones, we find our way.
Each glance a promise, softly speaks,
In hidden waves, our spirits seek.

Unseen Scribbles of Emotion

On crumpled pages, stories hide,
With ink that blurs where dreams collide.
A whispered thought, a fleeting glance,
In scribbled lines, we take our chance.

The heart's own ink spills on the page,
In quiet strokes, we break the cage.
What's left unsaid, we try to write,
In shadows cast by pale moonlight.

The Weight of Unspoken Words

In silence deep, a weight we bear,
Words trapped inside, a silent prayer.
Each pause between our breath conveys,
The depth of what our hearts would say.

Like heavy clouds before the rain,
Our thoughts linger, holding pain.
In quiet stares and distant sighs,
The truth resides in longing eyes.

Beneath the Muffled Heartbeat

In shadowed halls where echoes dwell,
A heartbeat whispers, strong but frail.
Beneath the hush, a story sings,
Of love concealed in fleeting things.

The pulse of life beneath the skin,
Binds souls together, thick and thin.
With every throb, an uncharted road,
Where every sigh becomes our code.

The Unheard Melody

In shadows dance the notes we miss,
An echo lost in the empty bliss.
Whispers float on a gentle breeze,
A song that plays with such sweet ease.

Each heartbeat strums a hidden chord,
In silence, truth is gently stored.
The world around hums soft and low,
A symphony we yearn to know.

Beyond the Veil of Words

In twilight's glow, the silence speaks,
It paints the gaps, as meaning peaks.
Words slip like shadows in the night,
Yet truths emerge in soft moonlight.

Each syllable a thread we weave,
Connecting hearts that dare believe.
Beyond the veil, our spirits soar,
Where love's true language seeks the core.

Soft Echoes of Sentiment

A whisper holds what eyes can't see,
Delicate hints of what could be.
Like petals falling to the ground,
In every silence, love is found.

Each moment shares a tender laugh,
In quiet joy, we find our path.
Soft echoes linger, sweet and pure,
In the hush of heart, we are secure.

Silence Speaks in Colors

In shades of blue, the stillness sighs,
A canvas painted without lies.
Golden rays kiss the silent air,
Illuminating thoughts laid bare.

Each hue unveils what words can't frame,
Emerging visions, wild and tame.
In the silence, a world is born,
Colors woven through whispers worn.

The Softness of Unheard Cries

Whispers lost in shadows deep,
Emotions buried, secrets keep.
Voices fade like distant sighs,
Echoes linger, unseen cries.

Hearts entwined in silent pleas,
Yearning holds a gentle breeze.
Tears like dew on tender leaves,
In the night, the heart believes.

Silent Caress of Longing

Moonlight dances on the skin,
A soft touch, where dreams begin.
Words unspoken, filled with grace,
In the dark, we find our place.

Timeless moments shared in glance,
Lost in depths of fleeting chance.
A silent vow, a breath of air,
Longing whispers everywhere.

Feathers on a Still Night

Night falls gently like a sigh,
Stars adorn the velvet sky.
Feathers drift on airy streams,
Carrying the weight of dreams.

Softly falls the silver light,
Cradling shadows, holding tight.
In the hush, where hearts take flight,
Feathers whisper of the night.

The Embrace of Quiet Understanding

In the stillness, souls align,
No need for words, our hearts entwine.
A glance exchanged, a knowing spark,
Together we ignite the dark.

Time stands still, the world aside,
In this moment, we confide.
An embrace that needs no sound,
In quiet, true love is found.

Whispers in Silence

In the stillness, secrets sway,
Breezes carry dreams away.
Soft murmurs touch the night,
Flickering stars, a gentle light.

Echoes dance where shadows dwell,
In whispers only time can tell.
Silent words, a fleeting chance,
Lost in twilight's silent dance.

Hearts entwined, yet worlds apart,
Unsaid feelings, a work of art.
In the quiet, hopes are spun,
Whispers blossom like the sun.

Embrace the calm, let silence speak,
In every pause, the answers peek.
Here in darkness, truths shall climb,
Whispers in silence, lost in time.

Echoes of Emotion

Every glance, a story told,
In every heartbeat, dreams unfold.
Laughter dances, joy takes flight,
While tears like rivers, grace the night.

A blend of colors, shades of fate,
Timeless feelings that resonate.
In the heaviness of despair,
Hope finds a moment to declare.

Moments linger, persist and flow,
In whispers, feelings deep and slow.
Echoes call from deep within,
Resonating where love has been.

Each thought a brushstroke on the heart,
In every silence, emotions start.
A canvas rich with hues that blend,
Echoes of emotion, never end.

Unspoken Brushstrokes

Upon the canvas, thoughts abound,
Colors whisper, softly sound.
Each stroke tells tales left unheard,
In silence, vibrant feelings stirred.

A palette rich with dreams and fears,
In quiet hues, the heart's true tears.
Brush in hand, a dance so bold,
Unveiling stories yet untold.

Lines and curves that intertwine,
Crafting visions, soft and fine.
Every hue, a heartbeat's plea,
In the art, the soul flies free.

Layers deepen, secrets blend,
In the silence, colors mend.
Unspoken brushstrokes, a silent song,
In creation's embrace, we belong.

A Symphony of Shadows

Notes of darkness softly play,
In twilight's veil, we drift away.
Shadows waltz across the land,
In silence, life's sweet music stands.

A haunting tune, the night unfolds,
Whispers of time that never grows old.
Echoes linger, a soft refrain,
In shadows deep, we feel the strain.

Conducting dreams, the stars align,
In the quiet, hearts combine.
A symphony in night's embrace,
Every shadow finds its place.

Together, we weave the night's design,
In every silence, the notes entwine.
A melody where shadows play,
A symphony of shadows leads the way.

Unwritten Letters to the Heart

In silence, words remain unsaid,
Upon the page, where dreams are bred.
A quill in hand, no ink in flow,
Thoughts dance like shadows, soft and slow.

Messages wrapped in longing sighs,
Promises linger behind closed eyes.
Each letter waits for love's embrace,
An unturned page, a hidden space.

Fingers trace where hope has been,
Each line a story, lost within.
A symphony of heart's intent,
In every pause, a love unbent.

Heartbeats in the Void

In the quiet, echoes resound,
Lost whispers in shadows abound.
Heartbeats stutter, a rhythm unclear,
A pulse that craves, a voice to hear.

Between the stars, where silence weeps,
The universe houses secrets it keeps.
Each beat a step into the night,
Searching for warmth, a guiding light.

In the vastness, connections arise,
Like constellations in endless skies.
Together in silence, we're not apart,
For every void holds a beating heart.

The Unseen Connection

Invisible threads weave us near,
In moments silent, true hearts steer.
A glance, a smile, unspoken ties,
Building bridges where silence lies.

Fingers brush past in crowded halls,
An energy pulses, when stillness calls.
What words can't capture, heart can know,
In the unseen, true feelings flow.

Time may part, yet love persists,
In the shadows, the spirit twists.
A bond unfelt, yet clearly seen,
In every heartbeat, love's serene.

Tapestry of Unsound Feelings

Threads of emotion stitched in frail,
A tapestry where words may fail.
Colors bleed into somber tones,
Each stitch a secret, each knot a moan.

Layer upon layer of time's embrace,
Fleeting moments, a fragile grace.
Silenced echoes in a woven maze,
Navigating life through a complex haze.

Frayed edges hide the tales of old,
In every tear, a beauty bold.
Unsound feelings in patterns wear,
A map of the heart, woven with care.

Beneath the Skin of Silence

Whispers linger in the air,
Echoes dance without a care.
Thoughts unspoken, hearts collide,
In the stillness, truth can hide.

Breath held tight in the night,
Lost in shadows, out of sight.
Yet beneath this quiet shell,
Lies a story weaves so well.

Fingers trace the lines of fate,
In the silence, we create.
Every moment, softly spun,
Underneath, the threads are one.

When the noise begins to fade,
In that hush, connections made.
Beneath the skin, where echoes meet,
Silence dances, bittersweet.

Fading Footprints of Thought

Footprints left upon the sand,
Memories fade; it's unplanned.
Each step taken, time will steal,
Waves wash over, dreams conceal.

In the dusk, shadows play,
Thoughts grow dim, drift away.
Like the tide, they softly swell,
Leaving whispers, none can tell.

In the silence, echoes roam,
Chasing dreams, far from home.
A fleeting glimpse of what has been,
Footprints lasting, yet unseen.

Still the heart clings to the trace,
Fading thoughts, an empty space.
Though the marks may disappear,
In our souls, they persevere.

Conversations in Colors

Brushstrokes dance upon the page,
Colors speak, the heart's stage.
Every hue tells a tale,
In their depths, emotions sail.

Red like passion, fierce and bright,
Blue like calm, a restful night.
Yellow laughter in the sun,
Green of life, where dreams are spun.

In the splatter and the smear,
Art unfolds our hopes and fear.
Vibrant worlds, a silent sigh,
In each canvas, we unwind.

Words can fail, but colors sing,
In the blend, our spirits wing.
Conversations without sound,
In the spectrum, love is found.

Where Words Fail, Feelings Thrive

In the silence of the heart,
Emotions rise; they play their part.
Words may stumble, thoughts may tire,
But feelings burn like inner fire.

A touch, a glance, a knowing sigh,
Lives entwined without a lie.
In that moment, nothing's said,
Yet a universe is fed.

Through the storm, we find our way,
In the stillness, love will stay.
Where words falter and fall behind,
Feelings flourish, unconfined.

So let us linger here awhile,
In the silence, every smile.
Where the heart can freely drive,
In this space, feelings thrive.

Emotions Unbound

In the shadows where whispers dwell,
Hearts collide, and secrets swell.
Every pulse a story shared,
Vulnerabilities laid bare.

Joy and sorrow, threads entwined,
A tapestry of the heart confined.
Laughter dances, tears may fall,
An orchestra that binds us all.

Moments fleeting, echoes long,
In chaos found, we feel so strong.
Waves of empathy crash and roar,
Emotions unbound, forever soar.

With every breath, the world expands,
Connection forged by gentle hands.
Embrace the ride, the highs, the lows,
In this garden of feeling, love grows.

Sculpting the Invisible

Chiseling dreams from shadows cast,
Molding hopes that fade so fast.
With each stroke, intentions clear,
Artistry born of quiet fear.

Hands move lightly, a gentle grace,
Carving light in a hidden space.
Visions appear, take their form,
Creating warmth amidst the storm.

A silent language, a touch divine,
Creating beauty from the line.
Sculpting life, we play our part,
In the gallery of the heart.

Invisible threads weave and bind,
In every curve, a truth we find.
Art reveals what words can't say,
Sculpted souls in bright array.

The Weight of Stillness

In quiet moments, time suspends,
A gentle pause before it bends.
Thoughts collect like heavy rain,
In the depth of silence, pain.

Breath held close, the world retreats,
Every heartbeat softly beats.
A sanctuary born from night,
In stillness found, we find our light.

Waves of thought, they ebb and flow,
In solitude, the seeds we sow.
Yet in the quiet, strength will rise,
From hushed whispers to the skies.

The weight of stillness, heavy, sweet,
A solemn dance, a heartbeat's beat.
Within the pause, the answers bloom,
In tranquil corners, we find room.

Fragments of Intimacy

Soft breaths shared in twilight's glow,
Unspoken words, feelings flow.
Glimmers of trust intertwine,
In every glance, a spark divine.

Fleeting touches, electric heat,
Moments linger, bittersweet.
In the distance, heartbeats race,
Fragments found in a sacred space.

Stories told in silences deep,
Secrets held that we must keep.
Hands entwined in gentle grace,
Finding solace in this place.

Through fragile threads, connections grow,
In soft shadows, intimacy glows.
A kaleidoscope of love's embrace,
Fragments cherished, time can't erase.

The Art of Imagined Touch

In dreams where fingers softly glide,
A canvas woven, side by side.
Each brush of skin, a whisper felt,
In silent worlds, our hearts weelt.

Colors blend in tender hues,
Crafting love, the mind pursues.
With every gaze, a pulse ignites,
In the dark, where hope unites.

Palette splashed with fervent sighs,
Moments held, like fleeting skies.
An ardent dance of what could be,
Imagined closeness, wild and free.

A brush of palm in twilight's glow,
As shadows stretch, emotions flow.
In the embrace of what's not seen,
The art of touch remains serene.

Intangible Embrace

In quiet folds of moonlit night,
We find our dreams take gentle flight.
A warmth that lingers in the air,
An echo of a love laid bare.

No need for words, just hearts aligned,
In spaces soft, where souls are twined.
A tender grasp in silence wrapped,
In gentle waves, our spirits tapped.

The pulse of life, a subtle thread,
In every glance, a promise said.
An intangible embrace we weave,
In every moment, we believe.

Through shadows cast and whispers light,
We dance among the stars so bright.
Together still, though miles apart,
In every beat, you fill my heart.

Gestures Beyond Speech

A glance, a nod, a knowing smile,
In silence shared, we roam each mile.
With gentle sighs, and eyes that meet,
We speak a language soft and sweet.

In fleeting moments, truths unfold,
In gestures warm, connections bold.
A touch, a laugh, a fleeting glance,
In simple acts, we find romance.

We paint our stories not in words,
But in the flight of unseen birds.
A world alive with gestures grand,
In every movement, we take a stand.

Through every silence, love is spurred,
In unspoken thoughts, our hearts have stirred.
In quiet ways, we come to know,
The depth of feeling that we show.

The Quietude of Affection

In stillness wrapped, we find our peace,
With every heartbeat, moments cease.
Whispers soft, like leaves that sway,
In the quietude, love finds its way.

The world fades in a soft embrace,
In silence, we uncover grace.
A gentle nod, a fleeting touch,
In simple joys, we feel so much.

Beneath the stars, where dreams reside,
With hearts Open wide, side by side.
In the hushed tones of the night,
Our love ignites, our spirits light.

A comfort found in depths unknown,
In silence held, we've truly grown.
The quietude of affection sings,
In every glance, the joy it brings.

The Weight of Breath

In the stillness of the night,
Whispers linger, soft and light.
Each inhale holds a secret deep,
While shadows dance, and silence weeps.

Caught between desire and fear,
A silent sigh draws you near.
Fleeting moments spiral away,
As dreams and wishes choose to sway.

Threads of thought weave tight and fast,
Echoes of a fleeting past.
With every breath, I feel the cost,
In the weight of what is lost.

Yet through the heaviness I find,
A fragile peace, a whisper kind.
In every breath, a tale unfolds,
Of hopes and fears, both brave and bold.

Interludes of Unexpressed Love

In the space where silence dwells,
Unspoken words cast gentle spells.
Each glance a chapter, eyes reveal,
The stories that we dare not feel.

Moments hang, like stars on strings,
Creating dreams of fragile things.
The heartbeats pulse in quiet tones,
Where love remains in whispered loans.

Every brush of hand's a sigh,
An unturned page, a quiet cry.
Memories captured, soft and spun,
In interludes, two souls are one.

Yet fear holds tight, a cloak of dread,
Words unsaid like ghosts in bed.
Longing lingers, a gentle thread,
In these spaces, love is fed.

The Space Between Heartbeats

Time pauses between each thump,
A quiet breath, a gentle jump.
In those moments, worlds collide,
Where dreams and fears are intertwined.

A heartbeat echoes, soft and slow,
Each pulse a tale that we both know.
The silence speaks in colors bright,
Illuminating hidden light.

In the gaps, a labyrinth hides,
Of thoughts unshared and ebbing tides.
Between each beat, a story grows,
In whispers only the heart knows.

So let us dwell in this embrace,
In spaces where love finds its place.
For in the silence, we can feel,
The depth of what is true and real.

Soft Footsteps of Emotion

Through the dusk where shadows blend,
Quiet steps of feelings wend.
Each footfall leaves a tender trace,
In the fabric of time and space.

The heart tiptoes, a wary guest,
In a world that never lets us rest.
Yet every step is laden gold,
With stories waiting to be told.

Beneath the weight of silent screams,
Whispers of love weave through our dreams.
In the air, sweet scents of hope,
Guide us gently, help us cope.

With every stride, we learn to dance,
To embrace the fleeting chance.
So let us walk on paths unknown,
In soft footsteps, we are not alone.

Unvoiced Connections

In the silence, whispers dwell,
Threads unseen weave their spell.
A glance conveys what words can't say,
In tender twilight, shadows play.

Hearts entwined in subtle grace,
Finding solace in shared space.
No need for loud proclamations,
Just the spark of kindred nations.

Tides of Thought

Waves of musings crash and break,
Echoes of dreams in every quake.
With every rise, a new idea,
The mind's vast ocean, clear and sheer.

Drifting thoughts like boats at sea,
Guided by currents, wild and free.
Fishing for meaning in the deep,
Where secrets linger, never sleep.

The Poetry of Presence

In fleeting moments, time stands still,
Life's essence captured, hearts to fill.
A smile exchanged, a breath, a sigh,
In presence lies the reason why.

Fingers brushing, a fleeting touch,
Words unspoken, yet felt so much.
In the here and now, we find our tune,
Dancing lightly beneath the moon.

Laughter in Liminal Spaces

Between the shadows, joy takes flight,
In whispered realms, laughter ignites.
Suspended moments, balancing grace,
Finding warmth in the quiet space.

Joy erupts where edges blur,
In the unknown, we gently stir.
Echoes of laughter shape our fate,
In the in-between, we celebrate.

Hues of Hope

In dawn's light, whispers grow,
Colors dance, soft and slow.
Petals bloom in gentle sway,
A promise brightens every day.

Through shadows dark, hope will glide,
With every tear, a light inside.
Brush of faith paints the sky,
In every heart, dreams will fly.

The azure skies hold secrets near,
Mirrors of love, wipe away fear.
Emerald leaves in silver rain,
Awaken life from silent pain.

In each hue, a story waits,
Of brave souls and open gates.
With every stroke, a world we weave,
In hues of hope, we learn to believe.

Gestures in the Gaps

In quiet moments, soft and free,
A glance exchanged, a melody.
Hands brush lightly through the air,
Silent words, a tender care.

Between the lines, our souls meet,
In pauses long, our hearts repeat.
A smile shared, no need for sound,
In every gap, love is found.

Echoes linger, softly fade,
While unspoken truths are laid.
In the space where hope resides,
Gestures speak where silence bides.

Together here, where shadows blend,
And gentle whispers never end.
In every pause, a story's told,
In gaps of time, our hearts unfold.

Pulse of the Unvoiced

In the stillness, a heartbeat flows,
Tales of the silent, where no one goes.
Whispers linger in the dark,
Flickers of light, a hidden spark.

Every shadow holds a song,
In quiet corners where souls belong.
The world spins fast, yet here we find,
The pulse of dreams, intertwined.

Lost echoes drifting through night,
Carried on wings of silent flight.
In every moment, a truth resides,
The pulse of the unvoiced abides.

Through the chaos, through the din,
Listen closely, let love in.
In every silence, a heart takes stand,
The pulse of the unvoiced, hand in hand.

A Palette of Dreams

With brushes soft, we paint the night,
A canvas rich, with colors bright.
Each stroke a wish, a heart's desire,
In every hue, we find our fire.

From twilight's shades to morning's gold,
In whispered tales, our dreams unfold.
The cerulean of skies above,
Reminds us all of hope and love.

In every color, a story we find,
A tapestry of hearts entwined.
With every shade, a journey's start,
A palette rich, a work of art.

And when the night swallows the day,
We'll paint our dreams in shades of gray.
For in the darkness, colors gleam,
In every breath, a vibrant dream.

Breath of the Unsayable

Whispers weave through silent nights,
Soft shadows dance in muted lights.
Unvoiced dreams brush against the skin,
Echoes linger where thoughts begin.

Glimmers flash in uncharted skies,
Secrets spoken with longing sighs.
Late starry hours hold the unknown,
In a world where the unsaid has grown.

Tender moments hang in the air,
Invisible threads bind joy and despair.
With every breath a truth to share,
Yet silence wraps what hearts declare.

Canvas of the Heart

Strokes of emotion paint the scene,
Where colors clash and blend unseen.
A palette rich with joy and pain,
Each hue tells stories time cannot feign.

Brush the edges with hues so bright,
Cover shadows with vibrant light.
In every corner, whispers unfold,
A tale of warmth in colors bold.

Layers of longing, pure and deep,
In the canvas, memories seep.
Each frame a glimpse of love's embrace,
Artistry rests in time and space.

Colors Beyond Dialogue

Vibrant strokes that speak so loud,
Painting truths in a swirling cloud.
Where silence crafts its own refrain,
And colors flourish, break the chain.

Brushes dipped in hues of tears,
Strokes of laughter, joy, and fears.
In every shade, a tale resides,
Beyond the words where feeling hides.

Fluid lines that bend and sway,
Capture moments lost in gray.
Beyond communication's grasp,
Colors speak where hearts unclasp.

Sentiments That Hover

Gentle breezes carry soft sighs,
Whispers linger under twilight skies.
Emotions dance like leaves in flight,
In the quiet glow of fading light.

Thoughts that float on fragrant air,
Sentiments weave through tangled care.
A whisper here, a shadow there,
Life's essence woven everywhere.

In the stillness, feelings blend,
Silent echoes never end.
Hopes that rise like stars above,
Sentiments that dwell in love.

Secrets in the Breeze

Whispers float on gentle air,
Untold stories everywhere.
Leaves rustle with mysteries tight,
Shadows dance in fading light.

In the stillness, secrets weave,
Nature holds what we believe.
Every sigh and every tone,
Keeps the heart from being alone.

Through the trees, a soft caress,
In the breeze, our thoughts confess.
Silent messages between,
Carried far, yet rarely seen.

Let the whispers guide the way,
In the dusk or break of day.
Every secret, every breeze,
Holds the truth that brings us peace.

Heartstrings Unstrung

Tugging soft at fragile threads,
Echoes dance where silence spreads.
Lost connections, muted cries,
In the depths, affection lies.

Once entwined, now drifting far,
Fading light, a distant star.
Memories hang like restless dreams,
Fractured hopes and silent screams.

Lonely notes in empty rooms,
Sorrow cloaked in quiet plumes.
Each heart beats a different song,
In the noise where we belong.

Though the strings may break and fray,
Love still lingers day by day.
Fragments of what once was true,
Remains in shadows made of blue.

Echoes of Silent Emotions

In the quiet, feelings bloom,
Creating space within the gloom.
Unseen tides pull at the soul,
Whispers share what makes us whole.

Time stands still, the heart takes flight,
Capturing moments, pure delight.
Each heartbeat echoes soft and clear,
Reminding us that love is near.

Words unspoken fill the air,
In the silence, hearts lay bare.
Though we falter, feel the weight,
Our spirits rise, love conquers fate.

Shadows pass, yet light remains,
In the echoes, love regains.
Silent emotions, ever true,
Binding us in a vibrant hue.

Whispers in an Empty Room

Four walls echo tales untold,
Silent spaces, memories bold.
Faded laughter lingers still,
Soft reminders, hearts to fill.

Dusty corners, shadows cast,
Moments cherished, long since past.
In the stillness, secrets glean,
Love once lived within this scene.

Every sigh, a ghostly trace,
Time remains in this lonely place.
Yet hope flickers like a flame,
In the silence, still the same.

Whispers float, a gentle sigh,
Love transcends the reasons why.
In this room, the heart will stay,
Carrying the past to day.

Colors Beyond Sound

In the shimmer of dawn's embrace,
Hues of hope and dreams take flight.
Feel the warmth of each bright trace,
　Echoes dance in morning light.

Painted skies of crimson glow,
Where whispers blend with shades of blue.
In every heartbeat, colors flow,
　A tapestry of me and you.

Through shadows deep and valleys wide,
　The quiet radiance will rise.
Harmony with time as guide,
A symphony beneath the skies.

　Unseen shades of laughter near,
　Every pulse creates a bond.
Listen close; the world is clear,
　In colors beyond, we respond.

The Pulse of the Unsaid

In the silence where thoughts collide,
Words unspoken find their place.
A heartbeat echoes, deep inside,
A bond that time cannot erase.

Moments linger, heavy air,
Feelings dance just out of reach.
In the stillness, we both stare,
Awaiting what the heart can teach.

Every glance a silent plea,
An unvoiced truth we dare not find.
In this space, we seem to be,
Together yet both intertwined.

The pulse of love is felt so clear,
In gestures soft, in tender sighs.
We discover what we hold dear,
In the silence, our heart replies.

Tracing Feelings in the Air

With every breath, the whispers soar,
Tracing dreams on winds that sway.
In the gentle night, we explore,
The language that words cannot say.

Beneath the stars, our thoughts take flight,
Fleeting glances weave a thread.
In the hush, we find our light,
A map of hearts in silence spread.

Each feeling caught in moonlit gleam,
A sketch of laughter, joy, and care.
We write our tale, a timeless dream,
In every moment, feelings share.

Drawing close, we etch our song,
On canvas vast, with colors bright.
In this dance, we both belong,
Tracing feelings in the night.

Unvoiced Whispers of Affection

In the quiet, where shadows creep,
   Lies a softness, tender, true.
Words unspoken, love runs deep,
   In every glance, I find you.

Gentle touches that linger long,
   Like a promise held so near.
In silence grows a sacred song,
Unvoiced whispers that we hear.

With each heartbeat, affection flows,
   Like a river winding wide.
In this dance, our courage grows,
   Together, with love as our guide.

In the night, beneath the stars,
We'll write the tales we dare to keep.
In unvoiced whispers, love is ours,
   In every secret longing, deep.

Half-Moon Conversations

Under starlit skies, we speak in hush,
With whispers soft, in the night's gentle crush.
The half-moon glows, a witness to our dreams,
In fleeting moments, it's not what it seems.

Time drips slowly, like dew on the grass,
Words weave like shadows, as minutes we pass.
Eyes twinkle bright, with secrets to keep,
In the quiet hour, our souls seem to leap.

The world fades away, just you and I here,
In half-moon light, there's nothing we fear.
Each laugh and sigh, a delicate thread,
Binding our hearts, where all fears are shed.

Dreams intertwine, like branches of trees,
In the warm embrace, we find our ease.
Half-moon whispers, a promise so sweet,
In this sacred space, our hearts gently meet.

Fluid Shadows of Feeling

Shadows dance lightly, in the fading light,
Emotions like rivers, flow out of sight.
Each twist and turn, carries stories untold,
In the hues of the evening, our hearts unfold.

Ripples of laughter, echo through the night,
While memories shimmer, in silver and white.
The fluidity of feelings, a gentle breeze,
Whispers of longing, float through the trees.

Time fades away, like mist in the morn,
In the tapestry woven, a new hope is born.
We ride the currents, of soft twilight's grace,
In the shadows, we find our own hidden place.

Fluid as water, our souls intertwine,
In the dance of the dusk, your heart touches mine.
Together we flow, like waves on the sea,
Embracing the essence of you and of me.

Echoing Without a Voice

In the silence, echoes arise,
Too loud to ignore, yet void of replies.
A heart left thirsty, in shadows it waits,
For words unspoken, to open the gates.

Reflections of thoughts, ripple like rain,
Each droplet a whisper, a shadow of pain.
Though silence surrounds, the message is clear,
In the space where we linger, I'm always near.

Questions hang heavy, in the air like mist,
Longing to be heard, but they fade into bliss.
The silence it cradles, my fears and my hopes,
In the quiet, I learn how to cope.

Echoing softly, feelings collide,
In the depth of the void, there's nowhere to hide.
A symphony playing, without any sound,
In the echoing silence, our hearts can be found.

Silent Stories in the Dark

In the darkened corners, tales softly creep,
Silent stories linger, in shadows they sleep.
Whispers of moments, unfold without light,
Each heartbeat a chapter, in the depth of the night.

Ghosts of the past dance, in flickering glow,
Memory's embrace, where tender thoughts flow.
Secrets are woven, in silence we trust,
In the dark's warm embrace, all doubts turn to dust.

Night wraps around us, like a soft velvet cloak,
In the stillness, even sadness awoke.
Yet joy finds a way, to sparkle and spark,
In silent stories that flourish in dark.

Together we wander, through unseen space,
Finding our truths in this quiet embrace.
With every shared heartbeat, our spirits ignite,
In silent stories, we bask in the light.

Echoing Ripples of Insight

In stillness found, a thought does grow,
Waves of wisdom, soft and slow.
Each ripple speaks, a story told,
In quiet moments, truth unfolds.

Reflections dance on water's face,
Memories linger, time finds grace.
Whispers echo, secrets shared,
In silent depths where hearts have bared.

A gentle hush, a pause to breathe,
In every silence, all believe.
Ripples fade, yet still they cling,
Lessons learned from everything.

So listen close, let silence sing,
In every echo, wisdom's ring.
For in these depths, pure insight stirs,
Life's intricate weave, in words and purrs.

The Uncharted Depths of Emotion

In shadows deep where feelings hide,
A tempest swells, no place to abide.
Waves of longing crash and swell,
In this vast sea, all is well.

Here currents pull, and hearts must sway,
Lost in the dance, the night or day.
Love's bitter taste, joy's sweetest song,
In uncharted waters, we all belong.

With every tear, a river flows,
In silent storms, the heart well knows.
To navigate through dark and light,
Is to embrace the hidden fight.

So sail the depths, embrace the tide,
In every wave, let truth reside.
For in emotion's vast expanse,
We find our lives, a fleeting dance.

Portraits in the Pause

In still frames caught, we breathe anew,
Moments linger, just me and you.
A silent glance, a whispered grace,
In every pause, we find our place.

Brushstrokes soft, like shadows fall,
Emotions bloom, in silence, call.
Portraits painted in the air,
Captured essence, love laid bare.

Time stands still, yet flows like streams,
In these portraits, we share our dreams.
In every pause, a heartbeat sings,
Creating worlds from simple things.

So let us dwell in quiet space,
Where stillness holds a warm embrace.
For in each pause, life's art unfolds,
In timeless tales, our story holds.

A Sonata in Silence

In quietude, the notes take flight,
A symphony born of soft twilight.
Each silence hums a vibrant score,
In hushed reverence, we explore.

Piano keys in muted hands,
Compose the music silence stands.
Echoes linger, phrasing anew,
In gentle tones, emotions brew.

Harmony found in breaths between,
Soft vibrations where dreams convene.
The world outside, a distant hum,
In silence, life's true rhythms come.

So let us pause, embrace the still,
In every silence, hearts can fill.
For in this sonata, calm yet bright,
We dance as one, lost in the night.

The Language of Unspoken Thoughts

In silence blooms a fragile word,
A whisper soft, yet deeply heard.
It dances lightly on the air,
A secret spoken, unaware.

In glances exchanged, truth lies deep,
In quiet moments, promises keep.
A story unfolds without a sound,
In hidden realms, emotions abound.

The heart knows well what lips won't say,
In shadows cast where feelings play.
With every pause, with every sigh,
The language flows, it cannot die.

So listen close to what is felt,
In every silence, love is dealt.
A tapestry woven, so sublime,
In unspoken thoughts, we find our rhyme.

Canvas of the Heart

On a canvas, colors blend,
Each stroke a story, each hue a friend.
With gentle hands, the artist paints,
A heartbeat's pulse, where dreamers faint.

Brushes dipped in joy and pain,
Creating worlds where whispers reign.
Each layer tells of hopes once lost,
The beauty found in quiet cost.

In every shade, a tale is spun,
A dance of light and shadows run.
With every splash, emotions flow,
In the canvas, hearts can glow.

The masterpiece unfolds with grace,
Reflecting life in a tender space.
In vibrant strokes, love finds its share,
A canvas of the heart laid bare.

Shadows of Tenderness

In twilight's glow, shadows creep,
Tender moments, memories keep.
A soft caress in evening's hush,
Where time stands still, the heart will rush.

Gentle touch in a fleeting glance,
In every sigh, a sweet romance.
Whispers linger in the cool night air,
Shadows dancing, love laid bare.

In fragile light, our secrets bloom,
Underneath the silver moon.
With every heartbeat, dreams entwine,
In shadows of tenderness, we dine.

So hold me close in this dim light,
Where tenderness is pure delight.
In every shadow, our souls align,
In this soft embrace, our love will shine.

Heartstrings in Solitude

In solitude, the heartstrings hum,
A melody soft, where dreams come from.
In quiet corners, thoughts take flight,
A symphony played under starlight.

Echoes linger in the stillness,
In each note, a hidden illness.
But with each strum, the soul finds peace,
In solitude, the burdens cease.

The heartstrings tremble, gently played,
Emotions woven, unafraid.
In harmony, we learn to heal,
In silence deep, our truths reveal.

So let the strings whisper their tale,
In solitude, our hearts prevails.
With every chord, a bond is spun,
In heartstrings, we are always one.

Emotion's Silent Palette

Colors whisper softly here,
In shadows of the heart's embrace.
Each hue a tale of joy and fear,
In silence, find the hidden grace.

Brushstrokes linger on the mind,
Where laughter dances with the pain.
In muted tones, we're intertwined,
The canvas loves, though not in vain.

Through storms of tears, bright shades emerge,
A symphony of quiet sighs.
In silence, all the feelings surge,
A rainbow forms beneath the skies.

With gentle strokes, the heart will paint,
A legacy of those we cherish.
In colors pure, and hearts so faint,
Our whispered dreams will never perish.

Beneath the Surface of Silence

In moments still, a world does weave,
Thoughts like rivers gently flow.
Beneath the calm, our spirits grieve,
Yet in that hush, new visions grow.

The echo of the unvoiced word,
Dances lightly on the breeze.
In quiet realms, hearts are stirred,
Finding comfort in the trees.

Through whispers soft of twilight's glow,
We sense the truths that lie in wait.
In silence deep, the mind can know,
That love can mend what hearts create.

So listen close, and let it guide,
The beauty in the breathless air.
For in the hush, we never hide,
But find ourselves, and we are rare.

Touching the Untouched

In valleys deep, where few have trod,
The untouched beauty sings anew.
With gentle hands, we brush the sod,
A sacred space where dreams break through.

Soft petals fall from ancient trees,
Each whisper tells a timeless tale.
In nature's arms, we find the keys,
To unlock hearts where hopes prevail.

With every step, we weave a prayer,
For moments lost, yet felt so near.
In silence shared, we deeply care,
For all the souls that wander here.

Together, we will find the way,
To touch the untouched, leave a mark.
As shadows fade into the day,
We'll dance anew, igniting spark.

In the Quiet of Presence

In moments when the noise will cease,
A quiet peace envelops the soul.
It's here we find our true release,
In stillness, we become whole.

The heartbeat whispers in the dark,
Each pulse a promise, soft and true.
In presence found, we leave a mark,
A gentle touch, a love anew.

With every breath, the world stands still,
In silence, we can hear our dreams.
A timeless bond, a sacred thrill,
In quiet spaces, life redeems.

So let the world around us fade,
In this embrace, be lost, be found.
In the quiet of presence laid,
We'll weave our story, rich and profound.

Meaning Beneath the Surface

In quiet depths where secrets lay,
A silent voice begins to sway.
Reflective waters, calm and deep,
Hold whispered dreams we dare not keep.

Each ripple tells a tale untold,
Of warmth and love, of hearts grown bold.
Yet shadows dance beneath the flow,
Where hidden truths may never show.

A flicker sparks, a movement clear,
Bringing forth all that we fear.
The depths conceal, yet also share,
A spectrum bright, both bright and rare.

So dive within, embrace the night,
For meaning often blooms from fright.
In hidden realms where silence gleams,
We find the strength to chase our dreams.

Threads of Yearning

In twilight's hush, the stars align,
With threads of gold, our souls entwine.
A tapestry of hope and tears,
We weave together all our fears.

With every stitch, a whispered plea,
For love to shine, for hearts to see.
These delicate strands, though worn and frayed,
Hold stories rich, in light displayed.

Through heavy hands and fragile hearts,
We seek the warmth that never departs.
In every fiber, passion glows,
A longing deep that softly grows.

So let us weave in twilight's grace,
With threads of yearning, we embrace.
In every knot, a promise bent,
A tapestry of love, well-meant.

Feelings in the Air

A gentle breeze, an unseen dance,
With whispers sweet that dare to prance.
The autumn leaves, they flutter high,
As feelings swirl beneath the sky.

With every gust, a secret shared,
Of hearts laid bare, of souls that cared.
The laughter lingers, light and free,
In every breath, a memory.

The clouds above, like dreams afloat,
Carry wishes on each note.
With every sigh, a hope takes flight,
Feelings rise like birds in flight.

So close your eyes, and breathe it in,
The feelings dancing on the wind.
In every gust, a tale to tell,
Of love and life, and all that's well.

Mute Melodies

In silent rooms where shadows play,
A silent song begins to sway.
Notes unspoken hang in the air,
Reminders of what once was fair.

Soft echoes drift where laughter lived,
Each moment shared, now tightly grieved.
A symphony of what was lost,
Mute melodies at tender cost.

With every heartbeat, a tune unsung,
In every corner, memories clung.
Though silence reigns, the heart still knows,
The depth of love that softly grows.

So let us cherish the quiet years,
In mute melodies, we shed our tears.
For even silence has its part,
A gentle song within the heart.

Milton Keynes UK
Ingram Content Group UK Ltd.
UKHW022007131124
451149UK00013B/1052

9 789916 907597